SWEETAPPLE EARTH

Also by John Heath-Stubbs from Carcanet

Collected Poems
Selected Poems

JOHN HEATH-STUBBS
Sweetapple Earth

CARCANET

First published in 1993 by
Carcanet Press Limited
208-212 Corn Exchange Buildings
Manchester M4 3BQ

A CIP catalogue record for this book
is available from the British Library.
ISBN 1 85754 004 2

The publisher acknowledges financial assistance
from the Arts Council of Great Britain.

Set in 10pt Palatino by Bryan Williamson, Frome
Printed and bound in England by SRP Ltd, Exeter

For
Adam Johnson

Acknowledgements

Acknowledgement is due to the editors of the following publications, in which some poems from this collection first appeared: *Acumen, Interim* (Las Vegas), *Outposts, PN Review, The Tablet, The Spectator, London Miscellany, North Wind, The Poetry Book Society Anthology*, 1990, 1991, *To Cast a Spell* (Orchard Books), *A Garland for Stephen Spender* (Edinburgh: Tragara Press), *Robert Greacen: a tribute at the age of seventy* (Dublin: Dedalus Press).

Contents

The Philosophers and the Pomes   1
Botanical Happy Families
    Nymphaeaceae   3
    Scrofs   4
    Solanaceae   5
    Violaceae   6
    Crucifers   7
    Labiates   8
    Drosera   9
    Campanulaes   10
    Umbellifers   11
    Orchidaceae   12
    Compositae   13
King Charles in the Bracken Stalk   14
London Magpie   15
A Summer Day   16
Midges   17
What Kind of Poetry?   18
Beautiful Railways   19
The Global Village   21
Household Notes   24
On Declining to Edit a Selection of A.E. Housman's Verse 25
A Cockroach Point of View   26
Seismos   27
Bulgarian Red   28
Pandora's Box   29
The Praying Mantis   30
Grave of an Amazon   31
Didius Julianus Imperator   32
Fallen Idol   34
Arthur Ransome   35
George Macdonald, 1824-1905   36
Goyesca   37
The Mulberry Tree   38
For Robert Greacen on His Seventieth Birthday   39
For Stephen Spender at Eighty-two   40
The Drunkenness of Noah   41
Not on the Palatine   43

Verse Useful and Ornamental

Phoenix	47
Sirena	49
The Ghost of Gruesome Towers	51
The Three Venturers	53
The Poets Laureate of England: A Short History	55
The Limerick Opera Festival	57
Mnemonics	62
The Two Robins	63
For Saint Valentine's Day	65
Written for the Visitors' Book of the Villa San Michele, Monte Selvino	66
Snail	67
For Shaun and Ursula	68
For a Fiftieth Birthday	69
The Toast of the Omar Khayyám Society	70

The Philosophers and the Pomes

(i)

A light Augustan breeze
Riffled through the leaves of an apple-tree
In a walled garden at Kensington
(A village not far from London). Isaac Newton
Sat in the latish summer sun. Diamond his dog
Was at his feet and snapped at flies. An apple,
As if already it had intimated
The coming on of autumn and of winter,
Quietly disengaged itself,
Leaving the bough it was suspended from. It fell,
Plummeting towards the centre of the earth,
As though filled with desire. Or was it not
Blind attractive force that drew it,
Just as the magnet rules the iron filings?

Newton observed. Out of his pocket
He took a small and tightly stoppered ink-horn.
Quills and paper were quickly brought to him.
Those quills of the wild goose
Began to scratch and scrawl, to scrawl and scratch,
Through days and months and years. The symbols
Crawled like ants upon the quires, until at length
The trumpet sounded, and the angels fell.
Unsinging now, the heavenly bodies
Whirled and twirled around through empty space
In a beautiful, just, intelligible order.

(ii)

Jean-Baptiste Lamarck,
On a republican morning, sat
In his Paris apartment contemplating
The living creatures, as they ascended
Towards the light, towards a full awareness
Of all their ambient world. The vegetative first –
The sponge, the polyp and the echinus.
Next come the sensitive,

1

With eyes on stalks and tactile tentacles:
The squid, the snail – or compound eyes
And quivering antennae: crustacean,
Insect, scorpion and centipede.
Lastly the intelligence emerges:
Intelligence a mere spark in the fish,
Vibrating in the serpent's quivering tongue,
Vocal in the birds, who at this hour
Chirrup outside his window, strong in the mammals,
From mouse to elephant. Above them all stands man,
With his five senses opened to encompass
Equality, fraternity, and freedom.

The plants dreamed on
In their green, peaceful realm, devising
Ever more complex and more beautiful
Foliage, fruit, and blossom. What then might hang
Upon the topmost twig? 'Well, let it be
This pear,' he thought, and picked one up,
From a blue faience bowl that stood before him.
A firm ripe pear, it was, the sun had fostered
Within a Normandy orchard. Deftly he pinched
The pointed end, and next pulled out the stalk
Which readily came away, and proved it
Ripe for the eating. Then he took
A silver fruit knife (mother-of-pearl its handle,
Its blade edged like the guillotine) and with a hand,
Which had performed so many nice dissections,
He quartered it, and so
Savoured the gritty sweetness of his world.

Botanical Happy Families

(A Garland for Dr Erasmus Darwin)

Nymphaeaceae

The white lily floats on the still pool
In places where the nymphs haunt;
The lotos dreams of nirvana; the yellow nenuphar,
Beloved of Mallarmé and the symbolistes –
But English peasants call it 'brandy-bottle' –
Hints, it seems, at another oblivion;
Victoria regia, enormous and imperial,
As the queen it was named for,
Displays itself upon the tropic lakes.

Long-toed, straight-clawed, spur-winged,
The lily-trotter, the elegant jaçana,
Goes across upon the lily-pads,
And seems as if he walked upon the water.

Scrofs

I dreamed I saw a yellow toad
Bent over her wheel spinning flax.
A tall fox, in purple gloves stood by,
Protending a precious bane.

Tight lipped, or gaping mouthed
A scarlet dragon snapped, while amazons
Rummaged in its maw for gold-dust or for sweetness.

Solanaceae

Falstaff thought potatoes aphrodisiac;
Tomatoes were called love-apples once.
Familiar and chaste enough,
They're now in every sandwich, every salad.
We also welcome to our tables –
Although a bit exotic still – the aubergine,
The pimento, the chili pepper (Becky Sharp
Found its name misleading, you'll recall).

But in the shadows stand
Sinister enchantresses, as belladonna,
Dulcimara, with the screaming mandrake,
Datura, bringing death or visions.

And there's a false friend too,
And that's tobacco.

Violaceae

'She never told her love' – the modest violet,
The sweet violet, or the blue dog-violet –
Types of unspoken passion. The heartsease too,
Deeply concealed in tussocks of long coarse grass.

But do they dream
Of tropical exotic places,
Where all the violet tribe are trees?

Here's a good, hard-working, honest family,
Packed with vitamins and purifying sulphur:
The cabbage after her kind – the brussel sprout,
The broccoli, the cauliflower, kohlrabi;
The turnip after his kind, likewise:
The mangel-wurzel, and the swede;
The radish, like a bright-faced schoolboy,
His elder brother, the harsh horse-radish;
Mustard too, and cress and oil-seed rape;
Wild garlic-mustard, which we name
Jack-by-the-hedge – what poets have sung you?
But I remember Juvenal,
Excluded from the rich man's dinner-party,
Going home to his garret, and his humble supper
Of boiled cabbage. But there are beauties too –
Stocks, night-scented stocks, and mignonette,
The wall-flower also. Do you want an Ovidian Myth?
I've got one for you here –
Victorian though it be and sentimental:
Once a lonely maiden
Was shut away from love in a high, strong tower.
In desperation she attempted escape –
Leapt from the window of her cell, but down she tumbled,
To lie, bruised and dying, upon the jagged stones.
The gods in pity turned her to a wall-flower:
It stands there still, beside the wall,
Red and blue and black, as were her bruises –
And no one ever asks her for a dance.

Labiates

Kit Smart's 'nation of living sweetness' –
Pre-eminently these, the Labiatae.
At our tables they are welcome guests,
Giving a savour to our meats, each with his own essence.
There's sage for stuffing pork, and thyme
(That's for the bees, who made Hymettus honey-mountain),
Basil, and marjoram, all kinds of mint –
Spearmint, peppermint, apple-flavoured mint.

Mentha was daughter of Styx. Upon the shore
Of the black river of hate she breathed a fragrance
Which souls who disembarked from Charon's ferry
Caught for a moment, as they trailed away
Into unending and despairing darkness.
Grim Pluto marked her beauty. That stern king
Became her lover, until Proserpine,
Forgetting her lost innocence among the meadow-flowers
Of Enna's field, found out the intrigue.
Demeter's daughter, now
The inexorable destroyer, had lost all pity.
She turned her rival into a plant –
A little sprig of mint.
Only the fragrance still persisted.

Drosera

'I'm sorry to have to do this to you,'
Said the sundew to the fly
As she devoured him. He'd mistaken
Her bright sticky droplets for clear points of dew,
And now was trapped. All his blood was drained away
By her digestive juices.
'You see, we're rather short of nitrogen
Down in this swamp,' the plant went on
'And you, being mobile, can get lots of it.
So I must eat you. It is just
Necessity, my dear.'

Campanulaes

Harebells are ringing on the upland heath
(They ring 'the bluebells of Scotland').
Brown hares engage in boxing minuets,
Run round and round in crazy circles.

Canterbury bells summon the pilgrims –
The last lap of their journey –
The holi blisful martir for to seke.

Umbellifers

They sport their delicate parasols,
Their Queen Anne's lace,
In woodsides, hedgerows, pastures, water-meadows –
Or did when I was young. Good friends are here:
The honest carrot, the yellow parsnip,
Fennel, and celery, and alexanders,
Carroway, dill, sweet cicely and chervil,
Pig-nuts, angelica, and blue eryngo
(Deep-rooted in the sand, prickly sea-holly).
And fleshy samphire, growing on the rocks –
St Peter's herb, for fishermen.

But yet beware the giant hogweed
Which scalds and burns. Cow-parsley too
Can be fool's parsley, and the hemlock
Is too much like the wild celery.
So fools can end up with wise Socrates.

Orchidaceae

Exquisite recluses of the forest –
An acquired aura of expensiveness –
Rich amateurs grow them in hot-houses,
Affluent tycoons present them
To their oh-so-costly women,
Who have not heard, or so I would suppose,
About the etymology of the name.

There's one that earns an honest living:
Her pods or essence in every house-wife's cupboard –
That one, did you know, is called vanilla.

I like our British wild orchids best,
(And so did Jocelyn Brooke, my friend –
A military orchid himself),
Playfully mimicking flies, or bees, or spiders,
Monkeys or man. But, best of all,
The spotted orchis. You will find it
In fields that have a chalky subsoil. This the true
Hyacinth of the Greeks I would conjecture.
The spots upon its leaves spelled out
The name of that poor youth, who died
Struck by the fatal misdirected discus.
Phoebus Apollo loved him –
Loved him for his white and slender body,
And, let's be frank (the Greeks were always frank)
His purple-pointed penis and his balls.
This orchid has its little phallic spike
Of purple flowers. Its bulbous root
Is like two testicles. Dear reader, that's
The etymology at which I hinted.

Compositae

The daisy Chaucer loved, and Wordsworth too;
The Scottish thistle ('no one
Injures me and gets away with it');
The Carline thistle, which an angel showed
To mighty Charlemagne, explaining to him
It had miraculously healing virtues:
Yellow Sow-thistle ('makes
Light and salutary meals
For rabbits' says the Reverend C.A. Johns –
Good old Parson Johns – his *Flowers of the Field*
One of my boyhood books! He occupied
A vicarage near Winchester, and there,
To keep away intruders,
He placed a notice in his grounds, inscribed
With this grim warning
BEWARE OF MANDRAKES AND OF CREEPING JENNY);
The China aster and the Indian marigold;
The fragrant Camomile, which likes being trodden on,
Napweed and, intensely blue, the cornflower –
A *deutsches Mädchen* in the harvest field;
Piss-a-bed dandelion, fleabane, groundsel, ragwort
(Loved by the scarlet and black
Day-flying cinnabar moth), strong-smelling tansy
Magical and divinatory yarrow;
Cooling lettuce, endive, chicory
And the two artichokes (one a sunflower –
Girasole not 'Jerusalem')
The other just an overgrown thistle;
The garden sunflower too, that stands up straight
Like a great gawky girl –
Clyte, who's had her head turned by the sun.

Each one not a single flower,
But a city of little florets
Lifted on a stalk towards the sky.

King Charles in the Bracken Stalk

'I'll show you something,' he said, and unclasped
His sharp penknife. Then, with a neat cut,
He sliced upwards the base of a bracken stalk
He'd pulled from the common where we sat.
'There is King Charles who's hiding in the oak-tree.'
I looked: my childhood eyes discerned
An intricate pattern of dark branching veins.
This could certainly be the Boscable Oak;
Not hard to make out among that ramage,
Skulking, a black swarthy fellow –
More Spanish-looking, they said, than English,
Who, disguised as a groom, had fled through Warwickshire
After the Worcester battle, fought and lost.

It did not seem strange creative Providence
Had stamped this royal eikon in the fern.
My father had always made it clear
What side I ought to have been on
During the Civil War, a loyalty
Subsequent Whig-historian-influenced teachers
Failed to subvert. Had there not been
A vague and ill-authenticated tradition
Some of our family helped in the escape?
But a lingering metaphysical paradox
Hovered in a six-year-old sceptic's brain –
If somebody had split a bracken stalk
Prior to 1651 – what then?
What would he have seen there? We'll leave that question
Unresolved till next Oak-apple Day.

London Magpie

Magpie, it's great to hear your chuckle
Among the streets and squares of my part of London,
Though you're bad news, I fear,
For the little singing birds I love so well,
Who are trying to rear their broods now, in treacherous April;
You and your flash brother
The jay, and your dingy cousin the carrion crow –
Egg thieves and baby-snatchers
All of you, corvid spivs.

A Summer Day

Sometimes when summer comes in England,
When sometimes it comes,
It is brave and Elizabethan, yet tender too,
Skies with the blue of butterfly wings,
And not the dragonfly brilliance
Of Mediterranean heavens:
High-riding crystals of ice, mares' tails, mackerel flecks,
Or flocks of little Bo-peep cumuli, or drifting bergs –
White castles where the Nibelungen dwell,
Jack-and-the-beanstalk giants, hoarding their treasures.

It is chop-cherry time, it is strawberry time, with apricots
Ripening on a southward-facing wall;
While the English too assume a sensual opulence –
Almost forget to be ashamed of their bodies.

So for a week, for two weeks, or three,
And then when the bubble breaks, and the thunder growl
We say 'The summer is over now – I told you it would be!
Too quick despairers, like Thyrsis and the cuckoo –
For not improbably there'll be more fine weather,
But brazen and blowsy now, with the oppression
Of the proud Caesar months, July and August;
And afterwards we'll know benign September,
Minting the beech and the field-maple to gold;
And saints will bless us with their special summers,
Those they annexe from winter –
St Luke with his balm, St Martin's charity.

Midges

This time of year, in early summer,
I sometimes find small itching bumps
About my ankle bones. It must be midges,
Midges that breed in the damp soil,
With just enough energy
To rise above the summit of my shoe, and burrow
Down through my socks, to get
That tiny drop of blood – it's all they need
Before they lay their eggs and die, ensuring
A good start for the coming generation.

I said midges, not midgets – but when I open
The Sunday papers, scanning the reviews,
To see which poets now are à la mode,
I tend to question the distinction.

What Kind of Poetry?

'What kind of poetry do you write?' asked the Bournemouth lady.
'I mean, should I understand it?' The pronoun 'I'
Distinctly bore a stress. And so I answered
'I really see no reason why you shouldn't –
All the words I use, or nearly all,
Are in the dictionary.' 'Oh dear,' she said
'That means I wouldn't understand your poems.'

Beautiful Railways

To A.J. with the works of Ronald Firbank

'Firbank's father makes brass bedsteads.'
'He doesn't, he makes beautiful railways.'
A prancing caprice he was, a vainglory,
A flower beneath the foot, an artificial princess,
And most of all, I think, that tragic cardinal –
Yes, I said tragic –
As the net of scandal and disgrace
Slowly closed round him, collapsing as he pursued
A choirboy through the precincts, a rosary
Hiding that which was meant to be hidden.

The great wind of the twentieth century had blown
The fig-leaves off the loins of all the statues –
In Valmouth, a suburb of Gomorrah,
A province of fairy-land. 'The Catholic church
Wouldn't have me, and so
I mock at her.' Ecclesia,
A silenced sister.

And yet it was in Rome that unaesthetic
Death grabbed him at last. He did not finish
With a charming sensation, but a desperate late night phone call.
'He'll be all right in the morning,' said Lord Berners,
'I'll drop round then.' And so he did –
The *signor inglese* had skipped away.

A final irony – presumed heretic,
He was interred in what had been formerly
The town ditch, but now prestigious
As the Protestant cemetery. All around him
The graves of young Englishmen who had died
On the Grand Tour. Anopheles,
Whining and flitting out of the Pontine Marshes,
Had given to them the last kiss.

And by the Pyramid of Cestius, repose
The dust of Keats, the calcine bones of Shelley.
When, at the end of time, those two bright stars
Shall rise again, he will rise with them –
A tinsel twinkle, a butterfly –
How easy forgiveness, and how astonishing.
('Little sly-boots, why can't they all behave?')
And so, with an accent mutated from Cambridge
Back to perceptible northern, he will go riding
Home to his Father's house on a beautiful railway.

The Global Village

(Homage to Charlotte M. Yonge)

'Write novels, and submit them for publication?
Well, of course I must insist
I should read through everything you write –
Read it, and, if necessary, censor,
And re-write it all.' Dutifully
She accepted her father's conditions,
And she did write novels, and they were printed,
And they were best-sellers too. 'As for the profits,'
He had also insisted, 'every penny, of course,
Must go to charity, to worthy causes.'
This also she agreed to. And so it continued.
After his death, the same control
Was exercised by Keble –
Keble the poet of the Oxford movement –
He happened to be her parish priest.

Hampshire was the county she was born in;
She died there too. It is a patch of earth
I also know well. So I imagine her
Going about her village of Otterbourn,
Full of good works, kind –
Not condescending – to the poor;
Writing her stories for young girls,
With a sharp eye for the small human follies
(Dramas transacted on the croquet lawn)
As Jane had had before in that same county
(But Jane's eye was clearer, her brushstrokes firmer,
Upon that little square of ivory).

Miss Yonge is walking beside a hawthorn hedgerow.
She stops to hear the whitethroat singing
Out of a nettlebed, and notices
The musk-mallow, that showy weed –
A Hampshire flower, a rarity elsewhere.

The phrase 'the global village'
Had not been coined in Charlotte's day.
But a trim ship, fitted and kitted out
From royalties *The Heir of Redclyffe* earned,
Was scudding amongst the South Pacific Islands,
With a crew of jolly Jacks, and a complement
Of sober-suited clergymen, all filled
With post-tractarian zeal to convert
Those lands where only man is vile, and in the hold
A cargo of bibles, books of Common Prayer,
Hymns translated by John Mason Neale
From Greek and Syriac, holy harmoniums,
Hassocks and cassocks, chasubles and albs.

Scent of exotic blossoms
Wafted on the balmy air. The palm-trees
Tossed their heads like the plumed heads of dancers.
The surf thundered upon the outer reef,
Gaudy with coral, where lurked
Scarlet-banded, deadly snakes, and fishes
Prickly and poison-bloated. A frigate-bird,
Long-winged, piratical, bright pelican-pouches
Beneath its formidable beak,
Tail forked, like an enormous swallow,
Was poised in the intense
Blue of a tropical sky. God's ebony children,
Hook-nosed and frizzy-haired, the Melanesians,
Flocked to the strange gospel. The fields
Were white for harvest.

Baptized, they still continued
To cultivate their yams, to collect
Their coconuts and pineapples and feed
Their grunting droves of pigs. But Long Pig now
Was banished from their menus. They'd exchanged
Cannibalism for early fasting eucharist,
Terror of ghosts and witchcraft
For sexual guilt, uncomfortable
Unnecessary clothes, subservience
To arbitrary, paranoiac chieftains,
For new white masters, giving some protection
Against marauding blackbirders, perhaps.

Miss Yonge was ageing now, pottered along
Her village street, and marked
How housemartins were still collecting mud
From puddles in the road, to build their nests
Under the gutterings of that church
She had collected funds for, and later on
Pears would be ripening on a southward wall.
I think the village children liked her – had she not taught them
Their A B C, their catechism, and some
Of Mrs Alexander's hymns? Christ's promises
Are for all. But, in her novels,
It might be someone who purports to be
A philanthropic lecturer from Bristol,
Who turns out really unreliable.

Household Notes

(i)

Emily it was, in Haworth parsonage,
Who made the bread. If you have kneaded dough
You'll know that you have got a living thing
Under your hands – and it fights back, fights back.
So, with firm fingers,
She squeezed the tumid viscous lumpish mass,
Infusing in it such suppressed emotions,
And so much pent-up rage, until she pushed it
Into the oven. Resurrected
As bread, it was, I fancy, no less wholesome
For all that passion consubstantial with it.

(ii)

A few years back, and southward,
In another parsonage, Cassandra Austen
Used to make mead, a good Hampshire tradition.
Real mead, you know, isn't a sweet drink –
The honey-sugar turns to alcohol.
With a little mace, and zest of lemon-rind,
It's sharp and lucid – rather like, I'd say,
A dry white wine, but it is wholly English.
On suitable occasions
Her sister offered it to visitors –
Or was it ordinary, just for the servants?
Behind the converse was a murmuration –
The ghosts of bees, in their straw skeps,
Annihilated at the summer's end
With sulphur, or with derris powder.

On Declining to Edit
a Selection of A.E. Housman's Verse

He sneaks up behind you, and kicks you in the balls –
Then runs away sniggering, fighting back his tears,
Having put on a false beard, ineffectually
Disguised as Quintus Horatius Flaccus,
Or a Shropshire peasant with suicidal tendencies.

But I've been to Shropshire also – the county
He never really knew, the sunset land
('Over the hills and far away'), until
The proud and angry dust reposed
Below the wall of the parish church at Ludlow:
The bitter scholar – girl students went away
In tears from his tutorials, yet he wept too
At the pathos of *Diffugere nives*.
At Ludlow now, the ashes call and cry,
Beneath the westering Pleiads,
To ashes under Uricon that do not answer.

A Cockroach Point of View

I suppose you hate and despise (I do)
The cockroach and his crew, who lurk
In damp corners of the scullery,
And venture out at night, to look for
Scraps of food (they prefer it rotten).
This they consume, and what they leave
They gleefully pollute. There is open war
Declared against them – poison-pellet, spray.

But surely we ought to look at it
From a cockroach point of view. It's a come-down
For those whose pedigree can be traced back
To the Carboniferous epoch, when the first
Amphibious pentadactyls struggled
Out of the mud, our ancestors,
With tadpole-tails they'd not yet discarded,
There in the primal swamp,
With giant club-moss, horsetails, and ferns:

A bit of a come-down, surely, for Archie the cockroach,
To scrounge a vicarious living from
An upstart naked ape, whose tenancy
Of this green world may shortly terminate.

Cockroach, so they tell us, is resistant
To radioactivity, and he'll survive
When all of us are done with. And now
Like throneless tsars, like Balkan monarchs,
They're standing by, the dictyoptera,
Ready to possess their world again.

Seismos

Seismos turns in his sleep and grunts a little.
In California hundreds die,
Fives of hundreds, thousands,
In China, Mexico, or else Armenia;

As once in Lisbon, baroque and gothic churches
Tumbled on worshippers who kneeled to pray at mass;

Martinique – a lighted tinder-box,
One great scream, countless unfinished stories;

Messina (and they even rumoured
Satanists had crucified a pig).

This green sweetapple earth,
Which we corrupt with greed,
Esuriant maggots, could shrug us all off,
As once the trilobites and dinosaurs.

Journeying at night through Mediterranean waters
I saw the glaring eye of Stromboli
Red through the darkness. Horror gripped my vagus
(Though really when there's no light to be seen,
The mountain's orifice being all bunged up,
It's time you should start worrying).

This is the permanent, the central, fire.
On what a thin puff-pastry crust
We skitter about like beetles,
Or dance our precious bourrées and fandangoes.

Bulgarian Red

Last night we discussed a bottle
Of red Bulgarian wine – inexpensive,
From the local off-licence,
We found it satisfactory – why not, indeed?
Bulgaria, you know, was Thrace,
From whence the cult of Dionysus
Infiltrated the Hellenic lands.
Lord of possession, master of dancing tragedy,
The swingeing phallic cone-tipped rod,
The ripped goat kid, or the dismembered child,
Must, muscaria, toxic ivy-juice,
He fumed in the poets' brains.

I met a poet from Bulgaria once,
Back in the sixties, at a conference.
He had found difficulties in getting there,
Obtaining a visa for a western visit.
Usually, he said, he had to spend
Vacations somewhere on the Black Sea coast –
I don't remember what the spot was called –
But anyway, smiling, I thought a little ruefully,
It was most interesting, he added,
The place Ovid was banished to.

Pandora's Box

You know the story of Pandora's box,
Or think you do. When it was opened
Hordes of little demons issued forth,
The troubles that beset the human race
And still are buzzing round about the world,
And only Hope remained to comfort us.

No, that's Nathaniel Hawthorne's version –
New England, protestant, and puritan.
Hesiod told it first, feeding his flock
On the ungrateful mountains of Boeotia,
Knowing, only too well,
The age he lived in was the iron one.
The Muses met him, tricked in violet garlands –
This is the tale they taught him:
Indeed Pandora brought a sealed vase
Down from Olympus, but, when it was opened,
All the blessings meant for poor mankind –
Us her descendants (she, the Hellenic Eve) –
Drained out, were wasted and dispersed,
Useless and savourless as spilled wine,
And only Hope remained, a monster,
With falsely-gleaming, rainbow-coloured wings,
To torture and to cheat us all forever.
Grouchy old Hesiod – it is a Greek story.

The Praying Mantis

The mantis, type of hypocrisy
(The name means 'soothsayer') has the appearance
Of lifting hands to Heaven in supplication:
But they're not hands, they're formidable claws,
Shutting like a clasp-knife.
The mantis does not pray, it stalks its prey.

I've read of one that looks just like a flower:
The butterfly, among the sunlit glades,
Descends, on many-coloured wings – he's dreaming
Of sipping nectar from the heart of fragrance.
But then he's grabbed, consumed, his juices sucked.

The female spider, as you know,
Devours her husband, just as soon
As marriage has been consummated. But the mantis
Is more impatient for her wedding breakfast.
She eats her mate during the act of love,
And, starting at the head, works slowly downwards –
The shotten genitals a final titbit.

Before you start back, at another instance
Of Nature's cruelty, look in your heart –
Look in its very depths. Might it not be
This, for the male mantis, is
Ultimate pleasure, the ecstasy,
Once and for all, to which his whole life tended –
His small unfallen life among the leaves?

Grave of an Amazon

Feminine the contour of those bones
The barrow had concealed – scattered around them
All the things she had loved best:
Her chariot of war, her spear, her buckler,
Her bow, and sharpened arrow-heads.

Not fabled then, those terrible women,
Ranging the Thracian and the Scythian marches:
No masculine child was reared, and they burned out
One breast of tenderness, the better
To draw a bow-string, and let fly
A whizzing shaft, that sang of death.

Nor framed in a mythology
Bright-haired Pentheseleia,
Upon the windy plains of Ilion –
She whom Achilles slew, and wept
That he had slain her, butchering Thersites
Because he mocked that grief.

Didius Julianus Imperator

'Daddy, you must buy it!'
How his daughters, his daughters and his wife
Egged him on, 'You must buy it, Daddy!'
They meant, of course, the Roman Empire.

The Praetorian guard, having disposed
Of the last unlucky incumbent, had decided
To put the whole caboodle up for auction –
Sale to the highest bidder. He could afford it too.
He'd made his pile, this acquisitive man,
Exporting savoury fish sauce
To all the further provinces;
And from the blood and bruised backs of the slaves,
Groans of the starving poor.

The gavel struck. He paid down cash
(It jingled with a kind of hollow laughter),
Assumed the purple, made a few
Tedious speeches to the somnolent
And ineffectual Senate. Before the year was out
He'd gone the way of all the others. The Praetorians
Notched up another tally.

'The world at sale' – no, not really the world,
Merely the fringe of a Mediterranean fish-pond.
In the high Andes, Guatemalan forests,
Beside the Yangtze or the Brahmaputra,
Other great states, each one claiming
That it was universal, tottered onwards,
Oblivious of Rome, towards
Their own inevitable disintegration.

As for his wife and daughters, I don't suppose
History has any news of them.
I like to think that they perhaps retired
To the Roman equivalent of a private hotel
In some salubrious resort – Baiae for instance –
And bored the other guests with detailed anecdotes
About the reign of mighty Didius.
We only know of it distilled,
A few brief sentences
Where we may savour Gibbon's irony,
While still great empires fall about our ears.

Fallen Idol

He stood on his plinth, he looked over the city:
The young people gazed up at him, and loved him, it seemed.
The bridegroom and his bride,
Formally united in the Palace of Matrimony,
Came to the front of his plinth, to ask
The idol's blessing on their union. The school-kids
Sang how he lived forever, and walked among them:
He kept, in safety kept them,
His little Komsomol lambs. High over all,
Rather like Oscar Wilde's prince,
Though not so pretty. That poor prince lost,
Leaf by leaf, his golden lingerie.
This one, rather suddenly, fell out of fashion.
One day he was toppled, and crashed to the ground
In a cloud of dust, to the cheers of the multitude.
And no one noticed a tiny form,
Winged like a midge, but with a human face,
Slit Tartar eyes, a small pointed beard,
Fluttering bewildered through the dust –
From the core of the statue, its secret soul
(The statue's soul not the man's). It wandered
The barren places of the earth, until
It saw before it a great effigy –
Two other forms beside it, human perhaps,
Or merely rough-hewn pillars. Then the colossus,
Seeming as if it recognised that small bewildered soul,
Relaxed its sneer into a smile of welcome:
'Join the club,' it said. 'My name
Is Ozymandias, King of Kings. And these
Are two of my friends – they're called
Baal Melkarth and Baal Peor.
Your plinth is empty, but our colleague,
The Golden Calf, is waiting to take over.'

Arthur Ransome

He went to Russia to learn the language
For commercial reasons. He translated fairytales,
And embraced the biggest fairytale of all;
Met Lenin, married Trotsky's secretary, and then
He wrote a series of highly successful stories –
Middle-class children fooling around with boats.

George Macdonald, 1824-1905

When the water in the basin overflows, becoming
A stream that runs through a wood, when the flowers on the carpet
Are turned into real blossoms and the trees
Are human – some seductresses and dangerous
Some maternal and protective; when you sleep in an arbour,
Observed by the bright eyes of birds, till at midnight,
They come without faces, the dancers –
Those who in life wore masks, and now
Are condemned to be featureless; when a book in the library
Is partly here in our world, and part in another;
When the librarian's ghost is a raven is Adam;
When innocence is under threat from goblin troglodytes,
From corrupt courts, from hunting white panthers;
Maternal presences are concealed
In secret drawers in unvisited turrets,
At the back of the North Wind; when a fire of roses
Purges perception, and you hold,
Among those images, an unbroken thread,
And goodness is ordinary as having your breakfast,
As being fed a spoonful of porridge
By a woman both old and young – she is that Wisdom
Boethius knew, and Hermas.

Goyesca

That melody of Granados haunts me,
And Goya's painting too – the one that's called
'The Lover and the Nightingale'. El Majo
Is just a boy – sixteen or seventeen.
If he looks older, it's because of his clothes –
Heavy formal Spanish dress of the time.
'You'll grow into them, niño.' He is in love –
His great soft silly eyes stare out of the frame
At us spectators. On his left hand perches
A nightingale he's tamed, fluting and twittering.
The little bird doesn't know it's a captive.

The Mulberry Tree

'Good neighbour Michael Drayton, and you, Old Ben
Stepped up from London to our Warwickshire –
The air is balmy, so we'll drink tonight
Under my mulberry tree, and hear the chimes.'

But English April's treacherous. Good ale and wine,
However generous they boast themselves,
Lower the temperature. The lurking microbe
Is everywhere, and waiting for its chance.

Death's always bitter – and pneumonia,
Though not the worst, isn't a cosy end.
But this, at least, was after a good party –
Drinking with friends. And who wouldn't like to have been
A caterpillar among those mulberry leaves,
To catch some of the talk that drifted upwards,
And pass it on when one had turned a moth.

For Robert Greacen on His Seventieth Birthday

It's not over the hill, and then down,
As the vulgar cliché has it, and not necessarily
Uphill all the way, to the very end.
Christina said that, and she was wise –
But life had given her a stingy deal.

No, Robert, it's a steady tramp,
Over ground that can be a little rough,
With the light fading. And ahead of you
The mountain peaks, sometimes masked
By dark and menacing clouds, and sometimes
Shining, in a touch of the setting sun,
With an immense, an unbelievable purity.

So trudge on, Robert, with your poetry,
A faithful mongrel bitch, trotting beside you,
Or running in front, to warn you
In case somebody's coming – Wordsworth's dog
Had that accomplishment, as you'll recall.
Go on, in the strength of Ulster, in the name
Of the red branch, the red hand, and the rectitude.

For Stephen Spender at Eighty-two

That good grey cuddy, he's carried you well –
Eighty-two years, like eighty-two miles, is a fairish trot.
He knew when to stop, when the bright-haired angel,
With the incandescent sword, was blocking the path.
He saw that vision, though you may have missed it.

He begins to stumble now. He's ready for
His stall, that clean cool dark place –
Though the road still stretches ahead, no end in sight.

And you, Stephen, are invited to a party, perhaps –
To dance among the atoms of Lucretius,
The fiery motes, the little water drops.
Or a good sleep, is it, to wake in the morning
With a new road, new landscapes, and
That long-eared friend, ready at the door –
Spruced up and hippogriff-winged?
It doesn't really matter – the going is all.
To be crown over yourself, to have watched the hawk,
Of those who were truly great continually to have thought,
To have marked the small tragedy
Of a pipe, broken against the fireplace –
These things have permanence.

So it's forward now, in a gentle twilight:
Trot on, dunk, gee-up – clip-clop, clip-clop.

The Drunkenness of Noah

It was over then – the dove had come back.
For six weeks he'd been cooped up
In a floating box, on a waste of waters,
Suffering the stench of the beasts, their bellows and screams,
His termagant spouse, nostalgic
For the old life and her social position
Among her now-drowned neighbours, his three sons
In their sibling rivalry, and their sharp-tongued wives.

Now they all bundled out in the sunlight,
On Ararat's frozen top. The ark
Was soon set in a great block of ice.
Pilgrims, ascending that peak, in after ages
Saw, or thought they saw, a dark shape
Enclosed in a blue transparency. Now the beasts,
Reptiles and birds, dispersed to their own places.
Tamandua, armadillo and colibri,
Anaconda and oven-bird, all went one way:
Wombat, wallaby and frilled lizard,
Cassowary and brush-turkey went another.
The elephant lumbered to the Indian jungle,
And Loxodon trampled the African bush.
The penguins settled for the South Pole,
The auks for the North. Two tapirs
Kissed each other, and then departed,
One for Malaysia, the other for the Amazon,
Never to meet again. The camels
Sought out Arabia and the Bactrian steppe;
Llama and paca the Andean altitudes:
All as if they'd evolved there separately,
Completely forgetting they were in one ark.

But Noah was weary, and slipped away,
While his sons were busy parcelling out
The boundaries of the continents between the three of them.
Like a soul descending into matter, he dawdled
Down the declivities of Armenian mountains.
For how long was it? The abundant landscape
Seemed never tainted by encroaching flood.

The boughs of the trees ripened into blossom,
And then were heavy and golden with apricots,
Sanguine with cherries. And lower down
He came to a valley prodigal with vines.
Purple and emerald-green the grapes –
Of their own accord the vats seemed filled,
And foaming with must. They promised a respite;
They promised oblivion from the long nightmare
That he had dreamed through. Then a voice called him,
Called him by name: 'Sisudra',
(It seemed as if humming through his brain's dizziness)
'I am she of the wine booth – other
Appellations there are. One night in my inn,
That stands beyond the limits of the world
Each soul must spend – a night of refreshment
And kindly rest, till it goes on
Treading its journey to the final judgement.'
He drank her proffered cup, and then he slept,
Like Adam, ancestral within the garden.
And thus his sons found him – his sons and his grandson.
Canaan and Ham sniggered. The more conventional
Japhet and Shem snatched up a cloak,
Clicking their tongues, and averting their faces,
They hastily covered the limp, purplish worm,
From which, as sperms, they had come. But I will leave him,
Among the flowers and the fallen vine-leaves –
Oenanthe and ampelis, the vineyard birds,
Twittering about him. But the ground-base
Was an old man's innocent, stertorous breathing.
Fuddled with must-scented wine, the soul
Was now contented to slumber in matter –
While through his dream a psychedelic rainbow
Shimmered like the veil of the Mother of God.

Not on the Palatine

Not in hard marble of the Palatine –
Presence-chamber, ante-room, frontstairs, backstairs –
Nor in Herod's palace, where,
Incense-fed, a bluish-greenish flame
Gutters, but cannot mask the smell of blood –

Not there is love, but here,
Among the straw and stable-smells,
Where breath of cuddy and stot condenses
In the cold air, and Mary bends
Over her first-born son. The Deathless here
Assumes mortality, the Infinite is constrained
By swaddling bands of space and time.

Verse Useful and Ornamental

Phoenix

Over the hot Arabian sands,
   Or desert wastes of Tartary,
The phoenix flies upon the breeze,
   And perches on the incense-tree:

The sole one of her kind, who's lived
   Three thousand and six hundred years,
While empires rose and fell, whose stories
   Were written out in blood and tears.

Upon that tree she builds her nest
   Of cassia, sandalwood, and cloves,
And rarer spices she has gathered
   In distant Yemen's fortunate groves.

Then she begins to start her only
   Sad and sweet mysterious singing,
Which sounds more loud and then more softly,
   Among the barren places ringing.

And those who hear that strange wild music
   Echoing around the lonely plain,
Find their senses all distracted –
   Their hearts can never rest again.

Then from the sky comes sudden thunder –
   Her nest ignited by the flash,
The phoenix burns in ecstasy,
   To crumble into soft white ash.

And in the morning travellers come
   From north and south and east and west;
For they must sift the cooling embers
   Which once had been the phoenix-nest –

A Taoist sage who's come from China,
   Next whom a Celtic druid stands,
An Aztec priest, a black-faced wizard
   From Africa's sun-burnished lands.

With mantras and with incantations
  They sift, till they discern a form –
A small, white, feeble, legless creature,
  Only just alive, a worm.

What chance is there of its survival,
  So insignificant and weak?
But soon it starts to sprout bright feathers,
  Bud wings, and talons, and a beak.

Then they rejoice, for in those ashes
  Another phoenix has been spawned;
Another phoenix-age begins
  And for mankind new hope has dawned.

The Ghost of Gruesome Towers

I am the ghost of Gruesome Towers –
I haunt there, in nocturnal hours,
And do it rather well, because
This talent is, and always was
A kind of speciality
In our distinguished family.

My grandad was a hideous ghoul
Who came, I'm told, from Istanbul,
His wife, the Lady Hypermania,
A vampiress from Transylvania.
Her story has a tragic twist –
An interfering exorcist
Destroyed her in – I have to say –
A most ungentlemanly way.
He staked her through the heart – to boot,
He stuffed her full of garlic-root.

My father lived in Barking Creek;
And for six days of every week
He worked as an insurance clerk,
But in the evenings, after dark,
He turned into a wolf, and prowled
About suburban streets and howled,
And showed his fangs, so keen and white –
And several people died of fright.
At length, a copper, called Ben Pullet,
Despatched him with a silver bullet.

My auntie is a Bleeding Nun –
I'm told she gets a lot of fun
Through haunting a monastic grange.
She has a quite surprising range
Of gibberings, and sepulchral groans,
Weird wailings, and despairing moans.

My uncle Poltergeist, whose haunt
Is a posh West End restaurant,
Has lately gained a lot of clout
Through throwing pots and pans about –
Sieves, colanders and nutmeg-graters.
The affluent diners and the waiters
See knives and forks and table-ware
Go madly hurtling through the air –
He once hurled a whole dinner service
At Lady Aspidistra Purvis.

My nephew – who's a bright young spark,
And just about to make his mark
(For to go far he has been tipped)
Haunts a damp, gloomy, Gothic crypt.
He's slowly mastering the technique
Of the high-pitched, blood-curdling shriek.
He's just a Nameless Something now,
But soon he'll learn his trade – and how!

I know what you're about to say –
This haunting lark has had its day.
It's all a lot of foolish flummery,
Pretentious and outmoded mummery.
You think I'll never frighten you:
Well just you listen – 'Hoo! Hoo!! Hoo!!!'

The Three Venturers

The cormorant, that with cold gleaming eye,
Watches the turbulent sea and empty sky,
Who on a rugged cliff constructs his home,
And dives and re-dives in the boiling foam;
The bat, that at the coming on of night,
On leathery wing takes off in rapid flight,
Hawking for cockchafers and flies and gnats
And little moths – these are the food of bats;
The bramble bush, that by the woodland track,
Seems trying to rip your jacket off your back,
Clutching with his sharp prickles – once these three
Possessed the lineaments of humanity,
But lost them, just because they could not cope
With fate's reversals, and frustrated hope.

I'll tell their story – it may move your pity:
They were three prosperous merchants of the City,
Heroes, indeed, of private enterprise,
Who had their fingers stuck in many pies.
None were more comfortably sleek and fat –
Not Lord Mayor Whittington and his great cat;
But Fortune's turning wheel, as you shall see,
Foredoomed them, and ordained their misery.

These were the days when wool was England's pride –
Source of her wealth, exported far and wide.
Each Pennine sheep bore riches on its back;
Lord Chancellors perched upon a wool-filled sack.
Therefore in wool our venturers invested –
At length, in nothing else much interested.
So a big ship they ordered to be made,
Called the *Saint Margaret*, to extend their trade.
Her maiden voyage began – the wind blew free,
And sunbeams danced upon the welcoming sea.
Great bales of wool were stuffed into her hold –
Wool which seemed fairly aching to be sold.

But soon the weather changed – the waves rose high,
And lowering storm-clouds darkened all the sky.
A tearing gale from the Atlantic blew
The ship upon the rocks. Lost were her crew,
And all her cargo – wool so soft and white
Sank in the sea, and so was wasted quite:
Though kindly mermaids, seated on those rocks,
Saved some few scraps for knitting into socks –
Five pairs a piece for little squids to don,
Down in the depths, when winter cold comes on
(Mermaids themselves, since they, as you'll recall,
Are wholly legless, need no socks at all).

But when the direful news to London came
You can surmise our venturers' grief and shame.
Their credit gone, and all their stock destroyed,
They seemed to wander in a haunted void –
Haunted by shapes they had not learned to face:
Lean Want, and griping Debt, and pale Disgrace.
So, in due course, they lost their human features,
Transmogrified to three quite different creatures.

One turned a bird, that flies before the storm,
Steganopodous, pelicaniform:
A cormorant, beside the fatal rock
Plunging below in search of his lost stock;
And one a bat, that, through the daylight hours,
Skulks in damp caverns and in belfry-towers,
Only at nightfall venturing out of doors,
For fear lest he might meet his creditors;
And one a briar that, with sharp ruthless thorn,
Often from straying lambs their fleece has torn –
From wandering wethers too: the reason's plain –
He's trying to build up fresh supplies again.

There ought to be a moral to this fable:
But I can't think of one. If you are able
I'd rather have you work one out yourself
Before you put my text back on the shelf.

The Poets Laureate of England:
A Short History

(A Piece of Useful Verse)

Jonson, of most just renown,
First assumed the laurel crown;
Then Will Davenant, who had
Claims that Shakespeare was his dad.
Great John Dryden wore the bays
In King Charles's golden days;
Others followed, not so great –
Shadwell first, then Nahum Tate;
Nicholas Rowe, whose tragic bent
Prompted his *Fair Penitent*;
Eusden, of this tribe the least –
Nothing but a drunken priest;
Pert, good-natured Colly Cibber
(Though some termed him fop and fibber);
Whitehead (you recall that he
Helped Pope with the *Odyssey*);
Wharton (Tom), a learned man
And an antiquarian.
After that – I can't think why –
They appointed Henry Pye;
Then Bob Southey, who, at last,
Had lived down his radical past;
Wordsworth next – but, by that time,
He was scarcely in his prime.
After him came Tennyson,
On whose brows the laurel shone –
Bathos, hovering near, decreed
Alfred Austin should succeed.
Bridges (*Testament of Beauty*)
Took the office, as of duty,
Masefield, for a lengthy spell
Served, and did it middling well;
Then came Lewis (Cecil Day).
After he had passed away
Betjeman could not refuse.
Now, of course, we have Ted Hughes.

While endures the British realm,
Royal Windsor at the helm,
Still shall warble (kindly Fate
Permit!) its Poet Laureate.

The Limerick Opera Festival

The Marriage of Figaro

Though born with a bright silver spoon
In his mouth, he would learn none too soon:
   'Out for a beano
   Signor contino?
You would go dancing, but I'll call the tune!'

Don Giovanni

That night when the trap-door stuck fast,
In Dublin, we all were aghast,
   Till a voice from the 'gods'
   Started shouting the odds:
'Thank heaven, hell's full up at last!'

Lucia di Lammermoor

Lucia, the Lammermoor bride,
Was destroyed by her family's pride.
   Forced to marry a cad,
   She went stark staring mad,
And of multiple stab wounds he died.

Il Trovatore

The plot line of *Il Trovatore*
Is gruesome and garbled and gory;
   The music alone
   Can serve to atone
For this – frankly – quite terrible story.

Rigoletto

The Duke's hunchback clown had a pretty
Young daughter concealed in the city.
   But she ended, alack,
    Tied up in a sack –
She'd been stabbed, by mistake, more's the pity!

La Traviata

He loved her with passion. But she
Was persuaded to let him go free.
   Her attempt to be good
    Was misunderstood.
He spurned her. She died of TB.

Aida

A drama of dolour and doom
And Egyptological gloom:
   She, a captive and slave,
    He a tenor, and brave,
Both walled up alive in a tomb.

La Bohème

Rodolfo, the poet, and Mimi
Found life in Montmartre rather steamy.
   He met her one night
    When she asked for a light –
The music of course is quite dreamy.

Madame Butterfly

Lepidopterous young Cho-Cho-San
Made a dreadful mistake with a man.
   For trusting a Yank
   She'd her own self to thank
When she found she was left in the can.

Cavalleria Rusticana

Sicilian rustics won't pass
For chivalrous types, as a class.
   They use knives when they scrap,
   And they don't care a rap
If it's Easter day, after High Mass.

I Pagliacci

Laugh clown, and give them their fun.
Don your motley – the play must go on.
   There'll be jealousy, rage,
   And blood on the stage
Before this light comedy's done.

Faust

Faust went distinctly astray
When his youth was restored one bright day.
   He set off in a whirl
   To seduce a young girl –
But there was the devil to pay!

Carmen

Carmen – oh she knew the score –
Found life in the factory a bore.
    She was up and away
    With young Don José,
Whom she ditched for a toreador.

The Tales of Hoffmann

Your past loves all led to a crisis –
Stop codding us, Hoff, our advice is –
    A mechanical doll
    A sorcerer's moll,
A soprano with terminal phthisis!

Dido and Aeneas

Troy fell. He for Italy started.
Stopped off at Carthage. Departed,
    Misled by some witches –
    Cantankerous bitches –
And left the poor Queen broken-hearted.

Peter Grimes

His neighbours accused Peter Grimes
Of most reprehensible crimes,
    Because he had quarrels
    With middle-class morals –
The victim, it seems, of his times.

The Ring of the Nibelungs

THE RHINEGOLD

Alberich, dwarfish but bold,
Of the Rhinemaidens' treasure got hold;
   Forged a magical ring
   Which the gods' cunning king
Pinched, paying giants in gold.

THE VALKYRIE

Sieglinde found marriage a trap;
Left Hunding for Siegmund. Poor chap,
   He was doomed to the slaughter,
   And Wotan's fierce daughter
To a lengthy, but fire-engirt nap.

SIEGFRIED

Reared by Mime, Sieglinde's young son
Killed Fafnir the dragon, and won
   The hoard, with the ring
   And that sort of thing –
Brunnhilde as well, when he'd done.

THE TWILIGHT OF THE GODS

Siegfried, for that was his name,
To the Court of King Gunther now came;
   But got himself stabbed
   For the ring he had nabbed...
And it all ends in smoke and in flame.

Mnemonics

(i)

The lama with an 'l' that's single
(Hear his little prayer-bell jingle!)
  Is a Tibetan priest;
The llama with an 'l' that's double
(He can spit, and causes trouble)
  Is a Peruvian beast.

(ii)

James Thomson, first of the three,
  For his own good reasons
  Wrote *The Seasons*.

James Thomson (BV)
  Was melancholic
  An alcoholic.

Francis Thompson (with a 'p')
  Was mystical
  And papistical.

(iii)

Meaning a distorted face,
I maintain the word 'grimace'
Rhymes like that. And they are dimmies
Who insist on saying 'grimmis'.

The Two Robins

Feeding on worms and things like that,
And nesting among tangled bushes,
The robin's from a junior branch
Of the great family of thrushes.

Not just in spring, but when the snow
Lies deep, we hear his plaintive song:
A bold and hardy little bird,
He stays with us the whole year long.

His crimson breast seems tinged with blood,
And people say that it's because
He tried to shift the crown of thorns
When Jesus hung upon the cross –

A holy bird: it's sacrilege
To injure robins or their brood:
A pious bird, who strewed with leaves
Those babes, abandoned in the wood.

I learned this as a boy – and since
To harm them is accounted blame
(At least here in the British Isles)
Robins are often very tame,

And even fly into the house –
But then some people catch their breath:
For them a bird that comes indoors
Must be a harbinger of death.

The robin of the USA,
The *Turdus migratorius*,
Clearly a thrush, hops on the lawn
Just as the blackbird does with us;

Nor does he bear a sanguine stain
Upon his person, but instead,
The feathers on this robin's breast
May properly be termed brick-red.

When winter comes he does not stay:
Southward he goes on migrant wing.
Next year his cheerful song announces
His own return, and that of spring.

Americans can't understand
Why, in the verse of English bards,
They read of robins among snow,
And why they're on our Christmas cards.

For Saint Valentine's Day

Saint Valentine, who runs
A dating agency for birds in bush,
Looks down from heaven, and sees no glint
Of coming summer suns,
Of springtime not one hint,
But only freezing fog and snow and slush;
Not even the bold mistle-thrush
Can bring himself to clear his throat,
And muster the first note
Of his accustomed dithyramb of hope;
And all the other birds just sit and mope,
With never a chirrup, nor a tweet –
But you and I, my sweet,
Have loved, are loving, and will love today
Whatever ill-foreboding drearyboots may say.

Written for the Visitors Book
of the Villa San Michele, Monte Selvino

Staying in this place was fun –
Good food, good wine, good cheese, and sun.
Cetti's warbler's here, and she
Repeats her sutra constantly
(And in their cage the budgerigars).
When evening comes there are the stars
With the cicadas and the bats,
Bush-crickets – and, of course, the gnats.

Snail

That humble little gastropod
We call a snail, or hodmandod,
Has his own way of praising God.

For lodgings he can never lack –
Accommodation's on his back.
He leaves behind a shining track

Of mucuous snot. We, by this train,
Chart his slow wanderings on the plain.
Most commonly, it's after rain –

The damp air suits his single lung.
To rasp the green shoots when they're young
He has a toothed file for a tongue,

And thus incurs the gardener's spite.
I have said 'he', but that's not right –
Your snail is an hermaphrodite.

For Shaun and Ursula

(On the blessing of their union, 4 November 1989)

Here, beneath the Scorpion sign,
May your hands and hearts conjoin.
Hence, ill omens of the season –
Whiff of gunpowder and treason –
Hag and goblin, all obscene
Revellers strayed from Hallowe'en;
Most of all, be absent, you
Brash, discordant bugaboo,
Asmodeus – back to hell,
At my verses' fish-like smell!
But – it's just a rustic story –
From the gates of purgatory
Stream forth holy souls, released
In this misty month – to feast
On the sable blackberry,
For these thirty days, they're free.
Can you hear them sing? – the theme:
'Nothing Love cannot redeem
Is, no false step of the past –
Here below, while time shall last,
As the sun and planets track
Round the clock-faced zodiac;
And beyond, above, the free
Citizens of eternity,
Issued each with harp and crown,
Rank on glittering rank, look down.'

For a Fiftieth Birthday

You want a birthday poem – but what's in fifty
To prompt my muse when she is feeling thrifty?
Year forty-nine is full of rocks and shoals,
A seven-fold square that threatens voyaging souls,
But you've passed that: and three-score years and ten
Is set up for a sea-mark to us men –
But fifty's nothing. Though the years may run,
Just you enjoy St Martin's summer sun.

The Toast of the Omar Khayyám Society

(a paraphrase)

And, O my friends, at last when I am sped,
And underneath the clay have gone to bed,
　　Where sleep the sultan and the slave, and all
The nations of the long-forgotten dead,

Appoint a gathering, and, when you are met,
Think upon old Khayyam, your friend – but let
　　Your talk about me be in no wise tinged
With sad repining or with vain regret.

And when the saki comes, bearing in hand
A flagon of old wine, O joyous band
　　Drink to my memory. Some few drops perhaps
May trickle downward to the silent land.